WALT DISNEY's
Snow White
and the Seven Dwarfs

A GOLDEN BOOK • NEW YORK
Western Publishing Company, Inc., Racine, Wisconsin 53404

ong ago, in a faraway kingdom, there lived a lovely young Princess named Snow White.

Her stepmother, the Queen, was cruel and vain. She hated anyone whose beauty rivaled her own— and she watched her stepdaughter with angry, jealous eyes.

The Queen had magic powers and owned a
wondrous mirror that spoke. Every day she stood
before it and asked:
   "Magic mirror on the wall,
      Who is the fairest one of all?"
And every day the mirror answered:
   "You are the fairest of all, O Queen,
      The fairest our eyes have ever seen."

As time passed, Snow White grew more and more beautiful—and the Queen grew more and more envious. So she forced the Princess to dress in rags and work in the kitchen from dawn to dusk.

Despite all the hard work, Snow White stayed
sweet, gentle, and cheerful.

Day after day she washed and swept and scrubbed.
And day after day she dreamed of a handsome Prince
who would come and carry her off to his castle.

One day when the Queen spoke to her mirror, it
replied with the words she had been dreading:
    "Fair is thy beauty, Majesty,
        But hold—a lovely maid I see,
        One who is more fair than thee.
        Lips red as a rose, hair black as ebony,
            skin white as snow..."
    "Snow White?" shrieked the angry Queen. "She
must be destroyed!"

The Queen sent for her huntsman.

"Take Snow White deep into the forest," she said, "and there, my faithful one, kill her."

The unhappy man begged the Queen to be merciful, but she would not be persuaded. "Remember my magic powers," she warned. "Obey me, or you and your family will suffer!"

The next day Snow White, never suspecting that she was in danger, went off with the huntsman.

When they were deep in the woods, the huntsman drew his knife. Then, suddenly, he fell to his knees.

"I can't kill you," he sobbed. "Forgive me, sweet Princess. It was the Queen who ordered this wicked deed."

"The Queen?" gasped Snow White.

"She's mad with jealousy," said the huntsman.
"She'll stop at nothing to destroy you. Quick—run
away and don't come back. I'll lie to the Queen. Now,
go! Run! Save yourself!"

Frightened, Snow White fled through the woods.
Tangled branches tore at her clothes. Sharp twigs
scratched her arms and legs. Strange eyes stared from
the shadows. Danger lurked everywhere.

Snow White ran on and on.

At last Snow White fell wearily to the ground and
began to weep. The gentle animals of the forest
gathered around and tried to comfort her. Chirping
and chattering, they led her to a tiny cottage.

"Oh," said Snow White, "how sweet! It's just like a
doll's house."

But inside, the little tables and chairs were covered
with dust, and the sink was filled with dirty dishes.

"My!" said Snow White. "Perhaps the children who
live here are orphans and need someone to take care
of them. Let's tidy everything up. Maybe they'll let me
stay and keep house for them."

The animals all helped, and soon the place was
spick-and-span.

Meanwhile, the Seven Dwarfs who lived in the cottage were starting home from the mine where they worked. On their way they sang:

"Heigh-ho, heigh-ho,
  It's home from work we go..."

The Dwarfs were amazed to find their house so neat
and clean. They were even more amazed when they
tiptoed upstairs and saw Snow White!

"A gleeping sirl—I mean, a sleeping girl!" said the
Dwarf called Doc.

"She's purty," said the one named Sneezy.

"B-beautiful," sighed Bashful.

"Bah!" said Grumpy. "She's going to be trouble!
Mark my words!"

Snow White woke up with a start. "Why, you're not children," she said when she saw the Dwarfs. "You're little men!"

The Dwarfs gathered around her.

"I read your names on the beds," said Snow White. "Let me guess who you are. You must be Doc. And you must be Bashful. Then there's Sneezy, and Sleepy, and Happy, and Dopey...and *you* must be Grumpy!"

When Snow White told the Dwarfs of the Queen's plan to kill her, they decided that she should stay with them.

"We're askin' for trouble," huffed Grumpy.

"But we *can't* let her be caught by that kwicked ween—I mean, wicked Queen!" said Doc. The others all agreed.

That night, after supper, they all sang and danced and made merry music. Bashful played the concertina. Happy tapped the drums. Sleepy tooted the horn. Grumpy played the organ. Dopey didn't know how to sing or play a tune, but he was very good at wiggling his ears!

Snow White loved her new friends. And she felt safe at last.

But the Queen had learned from her mirror that Snow White was still alive. "This time," she hissed, "I'll finish her!"

With a magic spell, she turned herself into an old peddler woman. She filled a basket with apples, putting a poisoned apple on top. "One bite," she cackled, "and Snow White will sleep forever. Then *I* will be the fairest in the land!"

Next morning, before they left for the mine, the Dwarfs warned Snow White to be on her guard.

"Beware of strangers," said Doc.

"Right," said Grumpy. "Don't let nobody or nothin' in the house."

"Oh, Grumpy," said Snow White, "you *do* care! I'll be careful, I promise." She kissed him and the others good-bye, and the Dwarfs went cheerfully off to work.

A few minutes later, the Queen came to the kitchen window.

"Baking pies, dearie?" she asked. "It's *apple* pies the men love. Here, taste one of these." She held the poisoned apple out to Snow White.

Snow White remembered the Dwarfs' warning. "But what harm can a poor old woman do?" she thought. "And that apple does look delicious."

She bit the poisoned apple. Then, with a sigh, she fell to the floor.

Told by the birds and animals that something was
wrong, the Dwarfs raced back to the cottage. They saw
the Queen sneaking off, and they ran after her.

As storm clouds gathered and rain began to fall, the
Dwarfs chased the Queen up a high, rocky mountain.
Up, up they went, to the very top.

Crack! There was a flash of lightning, and the evil
Queen fell to her doom below.

But it was too late for Snow White. She was so
beautiful, even in death, that the Dwarfs could not
bear to part with her. They built her a coffin of glass
and gold, and day and night they kept watch over their
beloved Princess.

One day a handsome Prince came riding through the forest. As soon as he saw Snow White he fell in love with her. Kneeling by her coffin, he kissed her.

Snow White sat up, blinked her eyes, and smiled. The Prince's kiss had broken the evil spell!

As the Dwarfs danced with joy the Prince carried Snow White off to his castle, where they lived happily ever after.